RAHGOR REVIEWS

"I am a student from James J. Ferris High School, I just wanted to say how much I admire you and your story. I love the book it's so inspiring! The best book I've ever read! It's amazing to see someone work so hard going through that struggle. I have all the respect in the world for you!"

—**Jose Andres Araujo Almanzar** *(Student)*

"I just really want to say thank you to your book One23 because it really MOTIVATES me in life. When I started reading the 1st page it really caught my attention and I finished the book in just one day. I will never forget what you said, 'My locations is not my destination.' I will always remember that and all the advice that you conclude to be my motivation to succeed in my life."

—**Chriselle Mae Pacla** *(Student)*

"Rahfeal is an extra ordinary individual whose captivating storytelling skills and powerful memoir show us just what the human spirit can endure, overcome and triumph. Rahfeal is a real superhero of our time and his energy, words and actions motivate and inspire us to strive for greatness in our lives and for the world."

—**Karen Floyd**, *Founder of Symmetry PR Ltd.*

"Rahfeal Gordon is a man that who walks into the room and commands POWERFUL energy and persona! His smile, his words, his presence, his motivation, his peacefulness, his ability to uplift others and instill confidence. PRICELESS"

—**Lorena Mann**, *Vice President, Operation & Productions at Women In The World Media / Tina Brown Live Media*

"I could relate to Rahfeal on a personal level because of his goget it mentality but at the same time his way of showing that a healthy and spiritual lifestyle is just as important. More than just being motivating, Rahfeal's presentation also highlighted that we're all just human beings in the end. Very inspiring!"

—**Nordin Ben Allal**, *Director of Nordesign*

"Rahfeal Gordon with his broad grin and indomitable SPIRIT has overcome adversities of homelessness and abuse for which he asks no sympathy and makes no excuses. He ACHIEVES and he gives!"

—**Michael S. Brown, Sr.**, *Former Director of Educational Opportunity Programs at Montclair State University*

"Rahfeal Gordon has an enthusiastic energy always present with him. He has an impressive story that explains why he is the human being he is: very humble, excited about life, very disciplined and focused in adding value to the society inspiring other people. 'Your location is not your destination' was one of the main sentences

I remember from Rahfeal. He will continue to be very important for all of us! Keep on inspiring us Rahfeal!"

—**Miguel Dias**, *CEO Dreams, Worldwide*

"Rahfeal Gordon is living proof of human being's strength and endurance. His inspiring life story is like a rainbow after the rain; hardships are only momentary, and knowing that is the most liberating feeling in the world."

—**Fara Mohri**, *Founder of Mohri Films*

ONE23

THE COMPELLING MEMOIR OF RAHGOR

2ND EDITION

RAHFEAL C. GORDON

RahGor Publishing & Co.

ISBN: 978-0-9978311-0-8 (Hard Cover)
ISBN: 978-0-9978311-1-5 (Soft Cover)

RAHGOR

(646) 358-4966 -office
(646) 358-4878- fax
info@rahgor.com
www.RahGor.com
www.One23Film.com

Twitter: @RahGor
Instagram: @RahGor
Snapchat: @RahGor
Facebook.com/rahfeal.gordon
Linkedin: Rahfeal Gordon

DEDICATION

This book is dedicated to my brothers Janvier, Alfonso, and Isaiah

I can't stop and I won't stop
And to all those living in shelters, abusive homes, going through a struggle, and trying to find a way out of a dark place—PLEASE keep the FAITH and never take a day off seeking the light and love that is also seeking for you.

CONTENTS

"To think health when surrounded by the appearance of disease, or to think riches when the midst of appearance of poverty, requires power; but he who acquires this power becomes a MASTER MIND. He can conquer fate; he can have what he wants."

—Wallace D. Wattles

FLASHBACK WHEN I WAS YOUNG

In the beginning, from what I can remember, my life was wonderful. I was the oldest of four boys, and we lived with my parents on Weequahic Avenue in Newark, New Jersey. My neighborhood was known as the Weequahic section.

As a young boy, I attended Maple Avenue School, otherwise known as "Little Maple," from kindergarten to third grade. I made honor roll every cycle, and I remember receiving high-fives from my father when he read my report card. My mother would be so proud and say, *"That's right! My Rah is smart."*

Those proud moments of my parents made me so happy. The expressions on their faces motivated me to maintain good grades and achieve greater success in school. After I graduated from "Little Maple," I was supposed to attend "Big Maple" to start fourth grade. Instead, my family moved to South 10th Street off South Orange Avenue in Newark before the start of the school year, and I attended a different

school. Times were still good for us as a family because no matter where we moved, we were all still together.

While living on South 10th Street, my brothers and I were known as the Gordon Boys. We were always having fun together on our block, and since there were four of us, we didn't really have too many other friends. At the same time, the few friends we did have loved hanging out with us. We weren't destructive kids, but some people may still beg to differ. As young boys, we played traditional games such as freeze tag, hide-and-go seek, manhunt, wallzy, and the hood favorite game with bottle tops called "tops." Those were the days! When we were allowed to sit on the porch, my father or mother would give me a dollar to buy everyone ice pops, sunflower seeds, and dime juices.

As young boys, we played traditional games such as freeze tag, hide-and-go seek, manhunt, wallzy, and the hood favorite game with bottle tops called tops. Those were the days!

My mother and father were the best parents for my brothers and me. My mother cooked delicious meals for us every night, and on Fridays, my father would take our family to Pizza Hut in Jersey City. We would be so excited that once we finished eating at Pizza Hut, we would eagerly talk about what we would order the next time we came.

My grandfather owned an auto body shop in West New York that is located in the state of New Jersey, and my father worked for him. On weekends, my father would take us to the shop to see Grandpa and all our Hispanic friends. It seemed as if we were the only black kids in the area. I remember a funny incident where we thought that one of the fellas was African American, and he burst out speaking Spanish. It was in West New York that we experienced a culture other than our own.

We made some of the best friends in West New York. My father would visit the park on his lunch break and play basketball with me. All my friends would watch in amazement while cheering me on to beat him. It was as if I represented the youth, and the playground was our territory. No adult, not even my father, was allowed to come in and win any of the games we played.

My father would visit the park on his lunch break and play basketball with me.

While Janvier and I played basketball, Alfonso and Isaiah enjoyed gymnastics. They would draw huge crowds of people who watched in amazement as they did 50 back flips in succession. Likewise, people would crowd around Janvier and me just to see us beat everyone on the court. It was the spark of the Gordon Boys making their name in a West New York neighborhood that was only theirs for the weekend.

During the summer, my father would take trips after work to Chinatown and buy $200 worth of fireworks for the block. Our friends back in Newark would ask, "When is your father bringing home firecrackers?" It was something everyone anticipated. Whenever he returned with firecrackers, he wouldn't let anyone know until a day later.

For example, I remember one occasion where my father woke me up at 6:00 a.m. to go with him to work

on a Saturday. At the same time, my mother was diligently preparing us breakfast. She said, "Look at my two men getting ready for work." When we finished breakfast and headed to the car, my mother looked out the window and said, "Be good and I love you Rah." I yelled back that I loved her too. My father laughed and led me to the trunk. When he opened it, I saw all the fireworks. He removed an M-80 firecracker and lit it with his morning cigarette. Once it exploded at about 6:45 a.m., the entire neighborhood knew that Mr. Gordon had firecrackers.

Life was golden for my brothers and me. We would see family members on holidays, birthdays, social gathers, cookouts, and school functions. We were blessed to have two sets of grandparents to interact with and love. It was these moments that kept me smiling. But hard times were on the horizon, and one may wonder what went wrong.

MOMENT OF CLARITY

As I write these memories of my life, it hurts me to know that I always had the answer to a problem that could have been solved with constant love, attention, and affection.

The problems for my family slowly developed. I remember my father would sometimes come home late from work, and my mother would worry about his whereabouts. Now, this could have always been an issue, but at my age, I didn't pay it any attention. Likewise, during some weekends, my parents couldn't afford a babysitter, so I would have to watch my brothers while they went to work. It was difficult because at times we didn't have any food in the house.

I can recall a time when we were so hungry that I went into the refrigerator and found a roll of biscuits. We were not allowed to touch the oven, so we started thinking creatively on how to prepare the biscuits. I thought about heat sources and the alternatives available that could substitute as an oven. I debated using the radiator,

but when I inspected it further, it was too rusty. Then I considered a lamp that had no shade, and I began placing raw biscuits on the light bulb. I don't need to share with you the result of this experiment. As you laugh at my strategy, you are not alone. My brothers still crack jokes about my failed attempt to cook those biscuits.

At one of my birthday parties, my intoxicated father arrived unexpectedly. In front of all my friends and brothers, he beat me.

Around this time living on South 10th Street, there was increased tension between my parents which I could not understand. My mother and father would increasingly argue. My father would come home inebriated and high after work. My mother would start to disappear when my father came home which my brothers and I did not like. We had this fear about our father that was just was getting stronger and stronger. How could a man we loved with all our hearts begin to turn into a monster that we tried to dodge at every opportunity?

As I was growing older, I was soon able to recognize what was happening to our "happy home." My father was destroying our family. At one of my birthday parties, my intoxicated father arrived unexpectedly. In front of all my friends and brothers, he beat me. I was so embarrassed that I did not want to interact with my friends for the rest of the party. My mother and god brother came into the room where I was hiding and assured me that all would be fine. It was at that moment that I started to hate my father. I felt that he didn't like me and that he resented me. Now that I had recognized his pattern of behavior, I began to notice the blatant disrespect for my mother and his mistreatment of my brothers and me.

Soon, the problems of our family started to extend past the walls of our home. My brothers and I were continually embarrassed as my parents began to engage in fistfights and loud arguments in public, outside of our house, and in the hallways of our three-family home. Additionally, my mother began to follow my father when he left the house to see if he was cheating on her. She detested my father and told my brothers and me that we shouldn't be like him.

As children, we were scared every day.

A war zone had developed in the Gordon household. As children, we were scared every day. The unstable situation was too much for our little hearts to handle, but as the famous anonymous quote states, "What doesn't kill you only makes you stronger."

As time progressed, it felt as if a gray cloud was over our lives. There weren't any more Pizza Hut outings, the trips to Grandpa's shop became less frequent, and there weren't as many high-fives from my father at night. These memories were now replaced with yelling, fighting, and beatings. Once in a while, the gray cloud that loomed over our family would allow some sunlight to appear. When these sunny days came, my brothers and I cherished them because we knew that they wouldn't last forever. But on one particular day, the sunlight beamed its rays on my understanding which gave me a moment of clarity.

MY SON HOLD DEATH FOR ME

I remember my father was in an unusually good mood on a warm summer day. He was off from work and decided he wanted to do something with his family. However, before we went on this family outing, my father said we had to stop at the famous BBQ restaurant Brothers which was around the corner. Oddly, my father didn't want to walk; he insisted that we drive to Brothers instead.

"Rah, come with me to pick up some things before we head out."

I really didn't want to go because it was so hot and Dad's car had leather seats with no air conditioner. In fact, I am getting hot just reminiscing about the day. I hopped in the car wearing my shorts and t-shirt and immediately jumped out because the leather seat seemingly burned my skin.

"Dad, why don't you keep the windows down? It's hot in there!"

"Boy, get your ass in the car and be a man!" he replied. My father definitely had a way with words.

After driving down the street for a couple of minutes, my dad parked his car and began to exchange hands and conversation with some of his friends. My father returned to the car and gave me a simple smile.

"You good?" It was one of his normal phrases of conversation.

I replied with a nod, and he turned the car's ignition to head to Brothers. As we were travelling to the BBQ restaurant, my father began looking in the rear view mirror. I looked back and noticed a police officer following our car. My father was tense, but he seemed somewhat relieved because we were already in front of Brothers. He waited for about two minutes so that the officer could pass, and then he began to give me instructions.

I looked back and noticed a police officer following our car. My father was tense . . .

"Rah, I want you to hold on to something for me. I don't care who comes to this car, do not let them have it. Okay?"

"Yes," I replied.

"I want you to close your eyes and open your hands. Do not open your eyes until I tell you to," he continued.

I followed his instructions because I knew by the tone in his voice that he was serious. The light might become dim and the gray clouds might come early on this sunny day if I failed to adhere to his directions. When he saw that my eyes were closed completely, he began to pour small solid objects into my hand. He then closed my hand

and told me to grip the objects more tightly. Pleased that I had followed his instructions, he instructed me to open my eyes.

"I don't care who comes to this car, don't open your hand. And I don't want you to look in your hand either. Do you hear me boy?" he demanded.

"Yes, Daddy, I won't open my hand for anyone," I responded.

My father then proceeded out of the car and towards Brothers. I watched him disappear into BBQ restaurant, and I waited on my curiosity to take over. I began guessing what could be in my hand. I started playing with the pressure that I had on my grip and concluded that a little peek wouldn't hurt. I quickly opened my hand and viewed colorful tops that held white powder in a very small capsule. Now, I was considered a geek by my fellow classmates, so I started using context clues to determine what was in my hand. Suddenly, it dawned on me. These were the things that were on the poster in school that said, "Say No to Drugs."

I quickly opened my hand and viewed colorful tops that held white powder in a very small capsule.

"Drugs . . . Daddy . . . Daddy does drugs!" I remember saying to myself in the hot car.

As soon as I exclaimed my realization, my father ran across the street to get into the car. After he entered, he asked me to close my eyes and open my hand. I felt him take every capsule out of my small and sweaty palm.

"Did you open your hand?" he asked.

"No," I replied.

I immediately turned to stare out my door window. I couldn't look my father in the face because I just realized that he used drugs.

KIDz ON THE ROOF

After I realized what was being hidden from me, I came to the conclusion that not only was my father using drugs, but my mother was using them as well. I didn't tell anyone what happened because I felt I would be embarrassed and no one would believe me. Those were two things that I did not want to occur.

As time progressed, the gray cloud I felt and feared became darker. My brothers and I would watch our father beat our mother to the floor while he was looking for money. We would watch and hear them argue repeatedly over things that probably were not major issues. At times, we would fake that we were asleep so we wouldn't be mistreated by my father. It was a crazy situation that no child or young person should have to endure.

I vividly remember a Friday evening when my parents engaged in a huge fight. My mother was thrown into the door by my father who was high. As my mother tried to rise from the floor, my father hit her again. He attempted to get to the front door, but my mother managed to regain her footing and strike him in the face while he walked down

the hallway stairs. Filled with rage, he turned around and grabbed her by the neck. He ran her entire body to the door, and after slamming into the hard door, she fell in pain to the floor.

My brothers and I began yelling, crying, and panicking because my mother was hurt. As my father looked at her, he began to yell and called her all types of derogatory names. Suddenly, my mother, who seemed as if she was not going to lose this fight, retrieved a long meat knife. Despite blood running down her face, her determination and strong will remained.

My mother and father squared off in the middle of the kitchen floor. As my mother swung the knife . . .

My mother and father squared off in the middle of the kitchen floor. As my mother swung the knife, my father attacked her, but she cut his neck. He retreated and realized he was bleeding. He assailed her again, but she was quicker and sliced his forearm.

As my father attempted to leave the house, my mother dropped the knife and began chasing him. In the mix of it all, my brothers and I engaged in a long conversation with a friend I will call Silence. But as soon as Silence was finished talking to us, my father returned to the house instead of my mother. I concluded that my mother left the house because she was tired of my father beating her. She left us on that Friday night with a man who was cut on his neck with a butcher knife and had no remorse for hitting a woman he called his wife.

When my father returned to the house, my brothers and I were already in our rooms waiting to see what might happen to us. But our father told us to go to sleep because it was past our bedtime. I don't recall the exact time, but it must have been late in the evening because my youngest brothers went immediately to sleep. After a while, I finally dozed into sleep.

As sort of a brother hierarchy, our sleeping arrangement was that the two eldest brothers were on the top bunk bed while the two youngest were at the bottom. Early in the morning at around 2:38 a.m., I was awakened by a beating from our father. As he beat my brothers and me in our bunk beds, he screamed in rage.

I was hurt mentally, physically, emotionally, and spiritually. I tossed and turned asking, GOD, why me?

"Where is your mother?"

"We don't know," we frantically replied in unison.

Despite our genuine reply, he continued to beat us because he was so high that he didn't care if we were telling the truth.

The beatings continued for about an hour as my father relentlessly questioned us about our mother's whereabouts. Finally, the beatings subsided, we were sent back to sleep, and my brothers dozed. But who could go back to sleep with the fear of physical torture at any moment? I couldn't do it! I was hurt mentally, physically, emotionally, and spiritually. I tossed and turned asking, "GOD, why me?"

This was it for me. I couldn't live in this situation anymore, so I jumped down from my bunk bed and walked to the window. My brothers were still sleeping when I began to open the window and screen. As I began to climb out the window, my brother, Janvier, awoke.

"Rah, what are you doing?" he asked.

"I am running away to grandma and grandpa's house," I replied.

As I said this, Janvier watched me climb on the roof. I stood there with my arms stretched out looking down at the ground beneath me. I kept hesitating because we were on the second floor, and I was only about nine years old. I was small in size, so everything looked too high, but I felt no one was able to help me but my grandparents.

Right before I was going to leap, I looked back in the window and saw my little brothers sleeping.

Time passed slowly as I contemplated my situation and built the courage to jump. Right before I was going to leap, I looked back in the window and saw my little brothers sleeping. Janvier was still awake and decided to get off the bed. He ran over to me at the window, and I asked him to push me off the roof. Instead, Janvier gave me a look that only those who go through struggles with someone would be able to offer.

"Rah, don't jump. I don't want to push you."

I told him that the only way to leave this horrible situation was for me to run to our grandparents' house by jumping off the roof. But my little brother had a different view in mind. Immediately, he asked me to come in the house and told me that we would get through these hard times together. I felt his words so much that I didn't even second guess him. We were brothers and when we needed each other, we were there to support.

I came into the house, and climbed up to my top bunk. I then leaned over and hit my two little brothers on the bottom bunk (which made them angry), and I fell asleep.

Author's Note: Years later I went by this house and realized that if I had jumped, I would have never survived the fall. I would have probably died instantly. I am forever grateful to my brother for helping me the way that he did. Even though he was very young and may not have remembered the entire situation, he was a true brother in a moment of pain.

WHITNEY

At some point, my parents split, and my mother was left with four young boys. We couldn't live on South 10th Street anymore, so we started living with family members. We moved from house to house each week. Soon, we noticed how we would be in the park for hours and then fall asleep in the car. My mother played it off so well that we didn't realize we were homeless at first. It was when we began living in shelters and taking showers with people who slept nearby Penn Station in Newark, New Jersey, that I arrived at the conclusion that we were homeless.

We slept in almost every shelter in Newark. Those were some hard times. I remember rushing so we could eat at the soup kitchen before it closed. Likewise, our clothes were from the Salvation Army. I couldn't tell you what my style was, but I would go to school thinking I was "fly" (sharply dressed). I would have on purple pants, a green shirt, non-matching socks, and some knock off name brand boots. I had a Kanye West mentality for a homeless kid! "Can't tell me nothing!"

I remember one of the shelters that we stayed in when I was in the 5th grade. The shelter was located in downtown Newark, and it was called The Apostle House. During the holidays, the staff would arrange special events and dinners. To my great joy, we were surprised by Bobby Brown and Whitney Houston.

I don't remember the exact day, but it was around 4:00 p.m. at the shelter, and we were scheduled to go to the Terrace Ballroom in downtown Newark to the holiday event hosted by Whitney Houston and Bobby Brown. All of the shelter families boarded buses which transported us to the event location.

> It was like a dream to see a huge Christmas tree with hundreds of gifts surrounding it.

Once we arrived at the ballroom, there were other families present from various shelters in the city. Christmas gifts for us were all over the ballroom. It was like a dream to see a huge Christmas tree with hundreds of gifts surrounding it. When it was time for dinner, we were seated at a table that provided food we wished we could eat every day. Soon, announcements were made that Bobby and Whitney would be arriving within the next hour. One could feel the excitement in the ballroom, and everyone started talking with great anticipation about meeting the two worldwide celebrities.

Although my brothers and I lived in the shelter with our mother, I could only think about my father while we were at the event. He was an avid Bobby Brown fan. He always had us get Gumby style haircuts like Bobby Brown, and we always heard his music in my father's car. I thought it would be clever to stand outside the ballroom so that I would be able to get their autographs when they arrived.

After a while, a limousine arrived with the celebrity couple. I ran back inside the ballroom and yelled with excitement that they were coming. The families began to get noisy, and the anticipation in the ballroom increased.

The families began to get noisy, and the anticipation in the ballroom increased.

When the couple arrived in the ballroom, they mingled with folks and took many pictures with several families. But as the event was concluding, I still didn't have Bobby Brown's autograph for my father, so I ran over to their table and asked Bobby for an autograph. I told him how my father loved him and how I was going to be a star.

As I was telling him this, the couple's managers said it was time for them to leave, but Whitney insisted on staying until I got my autograph. I ran around looking for a pen and a piece of paper. When I came back, they signed the paper and smiled at me.

"You have such a beautiful smile," Whitney said.

After signing the autograph for me, Bobby and Whitney left the Terrace Ballroom to much applause. Personally, I was on cloud nine. Despite my young age, I recognized the enormity of what had just occurred. I had a conversation with two individuals who changed music, style, and had an influence on people's lives. It was an amazing honor that I will never forget!

PROJECT BABIES

Our final shelter was at the YMCA in downtown Newark. After our stay there, we moved to Prince Street Projects. Younger generations may not remember these projects in Newark, but if you have ever watched New Jack City or New Jersey Drive, you can imagine the environment. We lived in those projects for quite some time. Our family then moved to 88 Barkley Terrace, which were the smaller projects behind Prince Street Projects.

At Barkley Terrace, we lived in a one bedroom apartment without any furniture. There was a bed, but that was where my mother and her boyfriend slept. As a result, my brothers and I slept on black trash bags that held the clothes we received from the shelters. It was common for us to share the washcloths, towels, and clothes so it never bothered us.

There were also times when we washed our clothes in the sink and dried them in the oven. We used a wire hanger to hold our damp socks, and we placed them in front of the oven with the door down to dry the socks. On other occasions, we placed our underwear and socks on the radiator because its heat was always better than the oven

heat. However, this faster drying method was not without consequences; the radiator often left rusty lines on our undergarments.

Sometimes, my mother would not be able to arrive home from work prior to my brothers and me getting home from school. She would give me the welfare card to get food to eat. Instead, my brothers and I used the card to pick the apartment lock so we wouldn't have to wait for her to come home. My brothers and I always planned and strategized our daily survival. It was our street smarts on Prince and Barkley Streets that instilled us with the power to endure our family's struggles.

. . . my brothers and I used the card to pick the apartment lock so we wouldn t have to wait for her to come home.

During the time my family was living in the projects, I was in the 6th grade at Louis A. Spencer Elementary School. I was a smart student, and I was selected for the gifted and talented program. Specifically, the program was designed for students who demonstrated accelerated learning relative to the total student body. I was given a letter for my mother to sign so I could participate in the program. However, because of my mother's situation, she was unable to attend the required parent-teacher orientation meeting. I was hurt as I had worked hard to be selected for this program. As a result, my mother and I got in a major argument, and I told her how I didn't think she cared for me. I was so devastated that I could not feel happy with my life at such a young age.

My mother was hurt when I told her my feelings. She also told me that my father didn't care for us and he didn't want to be involved in any part of our lives.

"You're lying," I said. "I don't want to live with you anymore. I want to live with dad."

My mother directed me to the phone to call and tell my father that I wanted to live with him. As I stormed downstairs to the payphone, I remembered the famous commercial to dial collect, "1-800-C-O-L-L-E-C-T." I began to feel happy because I was sure my father would tell me to pack my things and that he was on his way to get me.

I made the call, and I patiently waited for the operator to ask my father if he would accept my call. To my surprise, his reply was, "NO." He would not accept my call!

"I HATE YOU," I yelled with frustration.

I waited another hour and called him again. This time, he accepted my call. I told him the situation with my mother and how I needed his support and love.

"Dad, can I live with you?"

"Not right now. I have my girlfriend and her kids," he replied.

That day was so painful for me. I felt lost, but I knew I had the brilliance of a genius while living in the gutter.

The incident was a life-changing event for me; I felt now that it was I against the world. I needed money, food, and a way to control the situation around me, so I started bagging groceries. Following school, I would immediately go to the supermarket to begin work. It became a daily routine just so I could eat because I knew I couldn't depend on my mother to provide such basic necessities for me.

I needed money, food, and a way to control the situation around me . . .

However, I started to have competition from the other project kids who desired to work as grocery baggers as well. I had to be smart. I had to be creative. I started thinking of ways to beat my competition.

I began running from school instead of walking with friends. I would often arrive at the supermarket a half hour earlier than the store opening time. Also, after careful analysis, I would take the express lanes rather than the general lanes. I recognized that on the first of the month, customers would have two carts full of food which ultimately reduced my flow rate of customers. If I bagged groceries in the express lane instead, there was easier work with a higher number of customers. Additionally, shoppers with fewer items generally meant they had more change available to give.

During our time in the projects, my brothers and I began to see things differently.

My strategy worked so well that I was able to buy groceries for my family. At times, I would make $30.00, and it would be sufficient to buy food to feed my brothers, mother, and her boyfriend. I felt proud to provide for my family. Besides my mother, no one else was doing it.

During our time in the projects, my brothers and I began to see things differently. While I was bagging groceries, my two youngest brothers ran drug bags for the local drug dealer. My brother Janvier was neutral to the different directions of my two youngest brothers and me, but he was often quiet and observant to what was happening. When I would come home, Janvier would give me updates on my younger brothers, and when we were all together, we would discuss these events. Most people wouldn't understand the mechanic of our world, but that is why my brothers and I were mostly alone.

VIBRATIONS OF AN ANGEL

As time progressed, my brothers and I developed health issues that were due to stress and abuse. While these experiences were painful alone, such health complications only made our situation more difficult. For example, Alfonso was placed on various medications because of his diagnosis. However, despite his health issues, he was a very brilliant and dynamic child.

An aunt that the entire family was close to passed away from cancer. The entire family was saddened, and we all expressed our grief differently in the situation. After the funeral, we gathered at our grandparents' home, and I sat on the porch just thinking.

Suddenly, I heard people yelling in the backyard. I ran back to the rear of the house to see the cause of the outburst, and I saw Alfonso venting with aggression, pain, and hurt. My family tried to calm him, but he just seemed to get louder. Alfonso stated he was leaving and would not return. He started towards the fence, and when he got closer to the gate, he ran in escape.

Immediately, everyone began yelling and some started to cry. I was near my grandmother at the time.

"Go get your brother," she said with a direct stare and a calm voice.

Without hesitation, I ran after Alfonso. We ran at top speed in the middle of the street before I was able to catch up with him. I grabbed and hugged him so that he couldn't escape. Suddenly, he collapsed in my arms, and his eyes began to roll to the back of his head as tears ran down his cheek. I fell to the ground with him in my arms.

Suddenly, he collapsed in my arms, and his eyes began to roll to the back of his head as tears ran down his cheek.

"No, Fonso, don't do this to me!"

I began yelling for help in the middle of the street while crying harder than I ever had before.

"Alfonso don't die. Come on!"

My mother saw us from a distance and started running. As she approached, I tried to hold Alfonso's tongue so he wouldn't swallow it, but when my mother arrived, she started pulling him to her.

"Stop Mommy, you are killing him. Stop please!" I yelled some more, but she held him as he was experiencing a seizure.

I broke down on the curb watching my mother hold her young son in the street. When the ambulance arrived, I walked back to my grandparents' house. My grandmother came out the back of the house, and I fell into her arms with tears flowing like a river down my face.

"I can't take it anymore Grandma."

"Rah, you gotta be strong. You are the oldest. Do you hear me?" she said as she held me tightly.

She whispered in my ear that I would be fine and that I needed to stand strongly because my brothers needed me. While the pain of the incident almost brought me to my own breaking point, my grandmother's words gave me the foundation to hold me up.

Once my grandmother and I finished talking, I went inside to be by myself. More family arrived and some family left.

However, the memory of the day with Alfonso vibrated my world.

COME WALK WITH ME

At some point, my mother couldn't handle rearing all four boys, so my father decided to become involved again in our lives. I was going into the 7th grade when my brothers and I moved in again with my father. But at this age and time of my life, the love I once had for my father was almost gone. The dark clouds and rain we experienced with him earlier in our lives were times that my brothers and I tried to remove from our memories. It was a place that I did not want to return.

At the same time, I never knew until my college years that there was an ulterior motive for my father's new willingness to support us. Figuratively speaking, my brothers and I were walking around with dollar signs over our heads. A single parent with four kids can receive benefits from the government. Nevertheless, despite this additional income, my brothers and I never received the necessary supplies for school unless we received assistance from family members.

When we moved in with our father, we resided at 58 Nairn Place, which was off Clinton Avenue in Newark. Our home had thirteen people living there to include me, my three brothers, my father, his girlfriend, her son, her three daughters, and her three grandchildren. Unfortunately, there was only one bathroom in the house. When everyone had to use the bathroom after dinner, a line actually formed in the hallway.

I transferred to Hawthorne Avenue School, and I began to research possible high school locations. I made many friends at school and within the community, and these friendships gave my life joy and excitement. We would have house parties and played various hood games that made time pass by quickly throughout the day.

She asked if I attended church regularly, and I replied that I did not.

One memory from this time in my life touches my heart. Deshae and Earl, two of my closest new friends at that time, went to church every Sunday. One Sunday, I met their legal guardian, Ms. Lyons, who was in her late fifties. She asked if I attended church regularly, and I replied that I did not. She told me that she would like to see me in church because it was "the place to be." I agreed that I would go the following Sunday with Deshae and Earl.

After that first Sunday, I attended Hopewell Baptist Church in Newark every week. I walked from my house to church each Sunday at 6:30 a.m. just so I could arrive in time for Bible School which started at 8:00 a.m. I only owned one suit and a pair of hand-me-down shoes, so I wore the same outfit to church every Sunday. When the suit needed to be cleaned, I washed it in the bathtub and hung it up to dry in my bedroom window. It was my only Sunday suit, and I was proud to wear it.

The walk to church was long during the winter and even longer during the summer. I wore my suit through winter storms and during summer heat waves. When I wore the suit, I was headed to church.

Since the walk took about an hour and a half to church in often less than desirable conditions, I sometimes questioned my reason for attending.

When the winter months brought heavy snow storms, I wore my favorite lumber coat that didn't have any buttons to keep me warm on the walk to church. Ms. Lyons, a church friend, and a church deacon questioned me about a coat, and I told them I didn't own one.

Early one Sunday evening, my friend Earl came over to my house to ask if I could come by Ms. Lyons's house. My father approved, and I ran down the block with Earl to her house. When we arrived, Ms. Lyons was waiting for me in the kitchen with the deacon from church. He was holding a bag which read "Perry Ellis."

Ms. Lyons and the deacon smiled at me as they handed me the bag. After reaching inside, I removed a brand new winter coat with a price tag that read $110.00. I smiled broadly while trying to remain humble and grateful. I hugged both of them. They commented to me that they were intrigued with my faithfulness to God at such a young age and noted how I attended church even if my friends did not. They prayed for me, and after thanking them again, I returned home with my new coat. I continued to walk to church in the winter cold, but now I did so with a new coat and a new way of being happy.

THE BASEMENT IN HOODAVILLE

My father was having difficulty maintaining our house at Nairn Place, and he felt that we needed a change of space. Additionally, we were too crowded with so many people living under the same roof in the smaller house.

As a result, we moved to Martins Avenue which was adjacent to Tremont Avenue in Newark during the middle of my 8th grade year. Specifically, the area was known as Hoodaville. We moved to a house that was directly across the street from the graveyard. It also had a great side view of Bradley Court Projects, better known as "Tombstone."

I transferred to Camden Middle School, and I soon made friends with people who are still some of my greatest friends to this day. I was still interested in sports, and I played on the basketball team with and against some of the nation's top basketball players of my generation. However, during the final months of my 8th grade year, my art teacher, Ms. East, involved me with the Art Club. As I became interested in art, my involvement helped me meet

the required standards to pass the high school exam in art. I was accepted as an art major.

In the beginning, I really enjoyed my high school experience. At the same time, I dreaded returning home after the end of each school day. I would find every possible way to stay away from home until it was time to have dinner and be by myself.

I was motivated by the sounds of hip hop, and I was becoming more connected with the lyrics of the songs.

When I was at home, I stayed secluded in my room just listening to music. I was a big fan of Biggie Smalls and Tupac. I printed the lyrics to their songs and posted them on my wall next to their poster pictures. I remember having Raekwon's purple tape bumping heavy in my speakers while waiting for the debut of Wu-Tang Clan's new video "Wu-Tang Forever" on MTV. The video felt like a movie to me when I first saw it on television. I was motivated by the sounds of hip hop, and I was becoming more connected with the lyrics of the songs.

One day, I was listening to my music when my father's girlfriend announced that Alfonso had been suspended from school. My brothers and I knew that our father was going to beat Alfonso once he returned home. We were scared for Alfonso, but it wasn't something for which we could prepare.

When my father arrived home and was told of Alfonso's suspension, he immediately went to Alfonso's bedroom and beat him profusely. My father stripped down Alfonso to his underwear and viciously hit his chest, back, and legs. It was extremely difficult to watch my brother endure this pain. We felt helpless. We were scared to help our brother because our father was our master. It was as if we were his slaves, and beating of slaves was common on the Gordon Plantation.

After my father beat Alfonso until he literally couldn't walk, he dragged him down the basement staircase. He instructed Alfonso to stay and sleep in the basement until he was told otherwise. Two dogs accompanied Alfonso in the basement, which had no heat and no bathroom. There was a bed, but that is where the dogs slept. There were a few old blankets too, but who knows where those came from.

We sometimes sneaked him food to eat if my father felt he wasn t worthy of eating.

Alfonso stayed in the basement close to a month and a half. His routine was to come upstairs, get dressed, go to school, come home, and go back to the basement. We sometimes sneaked him food to eat if my father felt he wasn't worthy of eating. Likewise, we often whispered to him through the chained basement door.

I sometimes blamed myself for this incident because I felt I could have done more to protect my brother. I would not wish a situation like this on my worst enemies. My heart hurt as a big brother and as a human being. At the same time, I was affected mentally, and the incident caused me to become increasingly rebellious.

LET ME SHOW YOU LOVE

During the time in which Alfonso stayed in the basement, my brother Isaiah got into trouble as well. When my father learned about Isaiah's behavior, he decided to implement the same punishment for Isaiah as he did for Alfonso. Now, only Janvier and I remained in the house while our baby brothers were in the basement.

But it wasn't long before Janvier and I joined our younger brothers in the basement as well. When I was sent to the basement, I could not understand how my younger brothers were able sleep there. I slept on top of the washing machine with my favorite lumber jacket. When we needed heat to fight the dampness and cold of the basement, we turned on the dryer for a few minutes and placed our head and hands inside.

My brothers slept on the floor or even slept in the car because we were able to get into the garage. During the long hours in the basement, my brothers and I would talk about our future and how we wanted to live. We all said, "I can't wait to get big!"

Conversations like these helped maintain our spirits. We were each other's keepers. We fought, laughed, played, and loved each other as brothers, but sometimes because of our dark circumstances, we couldn't enjoy our brotherly bonding the way other brothers probably did.

I was becoming tired and fed up with the continual abuse that my brothers and I received. I was a freshman in high school dealing with normal teen issues, and combined with the child abuse at home, I was hurting. However, through all of this negativity, I was still able to smile in public. I didn't want anybody involved or aware of my problems, and if I had an issue, then I was going to have to solve it. However, my father always had a way of trying to change this mindset.

I didn t want anybody involved or aware of my problems, and if I had an issue, then I was going to have to solve it.

My father called me in his room one day and told me that I needed to stay home from school to pay the electricity bill with documentation from the welfare office. I was resistant to his demand because I had not missed a day in school, and now he wanted me to just so I could do his job. I explained to him that I had a test, but he told me that paying the electric bill was more important than a high school art literature test.

As a result, I did not attend school, and I missed my test. I became angry when I could not pay the bill because I was a minor. I told my father what happened when he came home, but he insisted I stay home again the following day. He said he would make a call from work in order for me to pay the bill.

I stayed home from school for a second day, and I still couldn't pay the bill because of my age. I became very worried; my father had given me a task which I was not able to complete. He felt that I was the man of the house when he was gone and what he couldn't do I should handle. He always instructed me to be strong in my position and to never allow other people get over on me. Although he was abusive, he managed to instill me with life lessons that I still live by to this day.

Although he was abusive, he managed to instill me with life lessons that I still live by to this day.

At that moment, however, I was more focused on his possible actions when he returned home. Instead of watching television in the living room, I went to my room to listen and watch for his arrival. When he did return, he checked to see if my two brothers were in the basement, and then he went to his bedroom to talk to his girlfriend. After a few minutes, it became quiet in the house, and I began to think he wouldn't call for me. But I was wrong.

"Rahfeal, get your ass in here!"

I raised enough guts, poked out my chest, and walked to his room calmly. I knew what happened next would be contentious.

His rampage commenced. "Rah did you pay the light bill?"

"No Dad. I couldn't pay for it because of my age. They said it didn't matter if you called," I replied.

He gave a stare as though he was so disgusted with me and he was hurting just by looking at me.

"Why do you act like a bitch?" he yelled. "I tell you to do one thing and you can't even do that."

I looked at him and knew that I was finished with this man whom I called father. He told me to get out of his room, and my emotion began to spill over.

"I can't take this shit no more!" I yelled. I began to walk out of his room.

"What did you say?"

All I could do was go right back at him with words. "Leave me the fuck alone!"

Without hesitation, my father immediately ran my head into the side of the door and then into the hallway wall. I tried to run to my room, but I had stupidly locked myself out my own room. Suddenly, my father helped me open the door by ramming my body against it.

Everyone began crowding around telling me to stop, but my brothers were cheering me on.

Everything was happening so fast. After I was rammed into the door, I don't remember anything but seeing black. I started yelling and threw back my right fist which ended up across my father's face. My father hit the floor, and I instinctively jumped on top of him. I grabbed him around his neck and began suffocating him. Everyone began crowding around telling me to stop, but my brothers were cheering me on. My father tried to flip me over to get control, but by the time he tried, I was already loose from the tussle and started running for the door.

As I ran, all I could think about was getting to my grandparents' house. I ran as fast as I could, but before

I could get to the corner, I was out of breath. I sat in the street and watched as Janvier came running to me.

"Hey Rah! Yo, you knocked daddy out, but he wants to see you," he said.

My mind was running all over the place. I composed myself and headed back to our house with Janvier. When I got upstairs, everyone was there while my father was standing in the middle of the floor. He told me he loved me and that he didn't mean to hurt me.

After he apologized, he directed me to my room which I was more than happy to hear rather than his words of forgiveness. I turned on my CD player and began playing Biggie Smalls "Juicy." I felt good, and I believed that our family situation would now be different.

Later on, my father knocked on my bedroom door. I remember that "Picture Me Rolling" by Tupac Shakur was playing when I heard his taps on the door. He apologized again and gave me a hug. After a few minutes, his girlfriend's daughter walked past my room.

"You know this is my oldest boy? He acts up, but I love him very much."

She smiled with a puzzled look.

"The only reason you are saying this is because he knocked you!" she said.

I smiled and then went back to my room and blasted the Ready to Die album by Biggie Smalls.

"No one has never been as broke as me,
and I like that."

—B.I.G.

WHAT IS THAT WEIRD SMELL

As time progressed, my brothers and I enjoyed our freedom outside of the basement. We listened to music on the porch during spring and summer days while watching the beautiful view of the cemetery that scared us during Halloween.

At times, our father hung out with us on the porch and cracked jokes. He had his moments of being fun and full of life. We were able to see God in him when heaven seemed to be within our home. It was those moments that we prayed for so we wouldn't see the clouds forming that dimmed the heavenly light around us.

One day, my father pulled up to the porch and asked me to join him in his car. He was smoking his favorite Newport cigarettes. He quickly asked if everything was good, and I nodded in affirmation. He stated that he needed me to do a favor for him, and I asked what it was that he needed. By this time, I was a little man because after the fight, he showed me more respect and gave me space to grow. He

started with hesitation in his voice, and then he asked me to buy drugs for him from my friends that hustled around the corner. I was so shocked that I was at a loss for words. I thought for a moment before I responded, and I began to see him as a man fading away.

"No," I said with a tremble in my voice.

My father asked again, and I repeated my response a second time but with more confidence in my voice. I started thinking how embarrassed I would be if I bought drugs from my friends. What would they say about me? What respect would I have for myself if I did do it? I immediately jumped out of the car and went back on the porch, and my father drove somewhere else to purchase his street medication.

I started thinking how embarrassed I would be if I bought drugs from my friends.

A few hours passed, and my father returned to the house. It was late by this time, but it was the beginning of the weekend, so it was permissible to still be outside. My father went inside the house, and then returned to the porch to go to his hangout spot. He asked me to come with him, so I joined him in the car. When we arrived at his hangout spot that I had known for quite some time, I decided to stay outside. After a while, I went into the house and was greeted by faces I had never seen before.

As I sat on the sofa, I smelled this indescribable odor that made my nose twitch. Once the smell became the aroma of the house, people were walking around like zombies and talking wildly. I sat on the couch and acted as though I was watching television, but I knew what they were doing. I remember the quote that was told to me, "A smart man can play dumb, but a dumb man can't play smart."

My father came from out of the kitchen and asked if I was all right. I said I was, and then he went outside. He returned a few hours later and went back to the kitchen. Once he did his medication that consumed the air with a weird death smell, he returned and looked at me. He told me he was going home, but he would be back soon.

. . . he was actually leaving me in a crack house to rear myself.

When he left, I had a hunch that he did not plan on returning. In fact, he was actually leaving me in a crack house to rear myself. He must have felt that I was able to take care of myself, or maybe he thought I could focus on becoming a better man than he. Nevertheless, he made a point that he was through with taking care of me as his son. I was 15 years old when he left me at the place I eventually called home.

CANDY KINGPIN

After a while, I began moving from home to home. Deserted by my father, I had to develop strategies for my daily survival and to generate income. As a result, I commenced my journey as an entrepreneur and leader.

I didn't know too much about business plans and all the legal documentation that came with establishing a real business. But I still felt that I could be a businessman while in high school. I established a company called Infinite Productions. My first business project to create revenue involved hosting a bake sale after school. My first investor for this business project was my grandmother. She packed me and my team into her Cadillac and drove us to the bakery to buy cakes and cookies. The project was a huge success and we raised close to $112. We were rolling in money!

The business I started became a staple at my high school during my time there. It was through Infinite Productions that we were able to host trips when the School Board said they didn't have money to help us experience the things we

wanted. We hosted bus trips to the New Jersey beaches on weekends, went to the Great Adventures Amusement Park, and held barbeques. It was great.

As with all businesses, there were shortcomings and moments when things didn't go so well. When things were tough monetarily, I would meet with my mother, just a reminder that I wasn't living with her, and she would take me with a group of kids to ask for money at the entrance to various highways in Newark. We would get half of whatever was donated; the other half would go to the church that we were raising money for. In the beginning, I was embarrassed, but I really needed the money. I wasn't working, and as a teenager, you get tired of people picking on you due to how you dress or because you have no money to participate in various cool activities.

. . . as a teenager, you get tired of people picking on you due to how you dress . . .

After school, I would hurry to the bus and go meet my mother so we could head out. On one of those days, my best friend at the time was telling me how he also needed money. It was the first time I shared with him what I was doing after school besides trying to organize bus rides and bake sales. He tagged along with me to see if he could do it. After about 10 minutes, he sat on the side of the road and refused to go out to ask for money. I was incredibly embarrassed because he was my best friend and he wouldn't do it. Of course, a few more friends found out and I had to live with the fact that I was truly begging for money.

The last straw was when I decided to quit playing basketball because I was only getting my playtime with the junior varsity team. I had much more free time after quitting the team. So I went back on the corner with that group and did what I knew would help put money in my pocket. Maybe a few weeks later, my coach pulled up to the light before getting onto the highway and I knocked on his window to ask for a donation. Boy, were we both surprised. His expression held confusion and sympathy. Mine conveyed a sense of exposure and discomfort. He held up traffic to ask me a few questions and then said something along the lines of "he better see me back in that gym during the next season."

After that, I quit wearing wrinkled shirts with faded writing on them just to get a few dollars from begging for a church I never attended.

I had a large number of friends, and I was adept at keeping my personal life private. At the same time, I still had to confront the outside world after the school bell rang. I had a few close friends who were in a similar situation to mine, but they believed selling drugs was the remedy to their problems.

I knew numerous drug dealers, too, as I was growing up, because they were the celebrities . . .

I knew numerous drug dealers, too, as I was growing up, because they were the celebrities in the 'hood. They drove the fastest cars, had the hottest women, and wore the coolest chains. They gave us money to eat when my parents didn't, and they were the cheerleaders at our summer basketball games. To young boys who were poor, they were easy and available role models.

As a result, many of my old friends started hustling for big-time drug dealers, but I couldn't be involved with this

business and lifestyle. I didn't understand the mechanics of the success rate. I only saw two results: death or jail. Neither of those options was any motivation for me. Consequently, I began to lose my friendships with those whom I had considered close. I guess when a person needs money, friendship becomes a casualty in the drug game.

While their industry was illegal, there were many business lessons that could be learned . . .

Although I didn't work for the drug dealers, I still studied and conversed with them. I was interested in them because, in a way, they were entrepreneurs. While their industry was illegal, there were many business lessons that could be learned from these drug dealers from the hardcore inner city.

One day, I was approached by the "king" whom my friends considered their boss. The dealer had considerable influence in my area when I was growing up, and he had most of the young boys hustling in the neighborhood.

"All of your boys hustle for me. When you gonna get down?"

"I'm good," I replied.

He smiled as though he was happy with my answer. "You always been different than the rest of your boys. I ain't mad at that though, nah meen?"

I thanked him for the comment, and then the lesson started.

"You seem smart, little homie. You remind me of myself when I was young. I be watching you going to work, playing ball, and with your little brothers. You the oldest, right?"

"Yep," I answered.

"I want to give you something that will help you as you continue to do your thing," the king said.

I had nothing but time, so I relaxed and let him speak.

"I want you to take everything that you think is negative and make it positive. I know that what I'm doing isn't a real job in your eyes or to others around you. It's cool, though, because I don't think anyone would be doing this if they didn't have to. But you see how it is out here, so we gotta do what we gotta do. But check this, I know you've been watching what's been going on out here. Take what you see and make it work for you. If you don't like something, take it out of your studies and put something else in its place so it is substituted with a positive piece."

I understood everything the king was telling me. I had so many ideas that I started writing things down right then. He told me to make my city proud and always recognize the real from the fake. He also said to always deal with people who make things happen. After our talk, I went home and started strategizing my plan to be the kingpin of my city.

Once I jotted down all the negativity that I witnessed in my city, I began to substitute it with positive ideas.

Once I jotted down all the negativity that I witnessed in my city, I began to substitute it with positive ideas. He'd told me to be the boss and make money. That was worth considering: it's difficult to help people without money. I pondered on what I could do to generate income, and then it hit me.

Instead of being a drug kingpin, I could be the *candy* kingpin. I could make candy my substitute for drugs. Candy wouldn't harm anyone (except for their teeth), everyone wanted it, and nobody was selling it in school. After I had the idea, I jumped quickly on the opportunity.

First, I found a wholesale store that sold candy such as Skittles, Snickers, Kit-Kat, and Twix in bulk. Since I was buying the candy in large quantities, I was able to purchase it at a lower price so I could later make a profit.

Next, I began to substitute the other pieces of my business for what the king had described. My "city" would be my high school. My streets would be each floor in the school. The mayor would be the principal. The teachers would be the city council members. The police would be the security guards. Wherever I stayed, I would consider the location my honeycomb (that is, my place to prepare products).

Third, I developed and established my strategic distribution plan. I would have other students selling my product (candy). Each grade level, freshmen through seniors, would have two sellers. Likewise, each floor would have a runner in case one of my sellers ran out of candy and needed to be resupplied. This was often the case during lunchtime because there was always a line to purchase snacks.

Now, I had to be smart at times, because students were not allowed to bring candy to school, especially to sell for personal gain. As a result, I "paid off" all the "city council members" and "police" by asking all my teachers and the security guards the type of candy and snacks they enjoyed. I created a list and made sure they had their respective candy fix whenever I was selling in my "city." By doing this, I was able to avoid getting my bags searched when I arrived at school, and therefore, I was able to sell my products in all my classes.

I was as fair as the drug kingpin because I ensured that everyone on the team could eat (make money)—I even had a payroll. Each person who sold candy received 25 cents for each piece sold. In contrast, if he or she damaged my products, lost them, or got them taken by "city officials," the careless seller would have to pay me for the candy. If a seller didn't have the money to do so, he or she would have to work it off by selling my candy until the debt was paid.

> No individual is powerful, great, or respected if there is no confidence or promise in his word.

My business operated better than I expected. I made as much as $200 to $350 per day, which included money from my after-school job. Out on my own, I was able to make enough money to feed myself, purchase clothing, and go to certain high school functions. I was even able to buy my prom outfit.

I became a kingpin in the city of candy by combining book and street smarts. I achieved the same results as the drug kingpin who told me to make a change. Whenever I reminisce, it amazes me that I chose to sell candy instead of drugs. I was always around drugs, but still I turned away. You might think that I would get looked down upon for my choice, but in reality, the man that everyone looked up to respected me for what I was doing!

I kept my word to my street mentor, just like he'd advised me. No individual is powerful, great, or respected if there is no confidence or promise in his word. As I promised the king, I took what was negative in my city and made it positive for me in my own city.

Ultimately, the lesson is that you can turn anything around if you use your intelligence and available resources.

YOU'RE NOT SUPPOSED TO MAKE IT

During my final years of high school, my brothers and I lived together again in my uncle's home. Times were good for us; we had a roof over our heads, we went to church together, and we always had food to eat. My grandmother was still actively involved in our lives during our stay with our Uncle. She also made it clear that she could not over step any boundaries with my uncle because he was our legal guardian.

I was working at Johnny Rockets in the Short Hills Mall while still selling candy at school. Janvier attended Irvington High School and was a "ladies' man." He also enjoyed basketball, which he played almost every day. Alfonso and Isaiah were still in elementary school and attended a gymnastics program called "Flip City" at the Boys & Girls Club. The program kept them off the street, and it was something at which they excelled.

When my grandmother, Janvier, and I would pick up my younger brothers, their coaches would often praise them for their amazing talent. The coaches often spoke about the possibility of them competing in the Junior Olympics and flying to Europe with the Flip City team. We were all excited and thought it was their big break out of the 'hood. I was impressed, and I thought frequently about the great opportunity my younger brothers could have in another country.

However, the strict rules we abided by while living with my uncle precluded this opportunity for my younger brothers. As Alfonso and Isaiah progressed in the Boys & Girls Club, they spent less time at church. But our uncle would not allow any worldly activity to be prioritized over church. "If you live in my house, you will have to go to church," he repeatedly told us.

> "If you live in my house, you will have to go to church," he repeatedly told us.

While we understood this important principle, we were in church all the time. We were there all day on Sundays, as we participated in choir rehearsals and other youth activities. We appreciated my uncle's strong advocacy for church, but he was also strict about my younger brothers competing after school and completing their homework; his priorities left little time for theirs. Frankly speaking, my younger brothers were not as interested in church as my uncle would have liked them to be. They had a talent that could take them all over the world, and it was being restricted. The situation was a point of contention, and I struggled with the issue.

Ultimately, my grandmother had to removed my brothers from the Boys & Girls Club because she did not want to jeopardize our living situation with our uncle. As soon as this happened, my younger brothers were once again hanging out with the drug dealers. They began to skip school because they felt there was no longer any need to maintain their grades. The praise for the God-given talent they possessed had now ceased. They were now flipping for the neighborhood hustlers and friends to get 'hood respect.

After a while, the situation with our uncle began to unravel. Frustration and constant arguments were increasingly common. Finally, my brothers left school and became immersed in the lifestyle of the drug dealer. In a way, it was like watching an experiment. When positive tools and resources are stripped from a child who needs them to grow, other things will inevitably take their place.

When positive tools and resources are stripped from a child who needs them to grow, other things will inevitably take their place.

Within a year, I left my uncle's house and moved in with my grandparents to finish my last year of high school. I started thinking about college and recognized that it would be an opportunity to get away from all the hurt and pain I'd experienced. Given my experiences, intelligence, and even my tribulations, I believed I could be accepted into the top schools in the country. There were only two institutions on my list, Princeton University and Morehouse College.

When I informed one of my guidance counselors that I wanted to attend either Princeton University or Morehouse College, she laughed at me. She said that my high school grades would only allow me to gain acceptance into a community college.

I was a bit hurt by her lack of confidence in my ability. I had already completed the application for Morehouse College, and I was confident that I could get accepted. However, as I walked out of the counselor's office and onto the street, I went to the nearest garbage can and threw in my application. It is funny how most people don't know what they say to an individual can hurt his future or scare him away from his dreams.

PARENT & TEACHER NIGHT

College became more and more a topic of discussion when I was in my senior year of high school. I was involved in many school activities and doing what I could with what I had. It was an exciting time and I wanted to enjoy every last bit of it. I would do things like walk through the halls after school thinking about my first day arriving as a freshman. I would spend time talking with the janitors and lunch aides who served our food everyday. I really enjoyed my time at school because it was my refuge and safe haven. I could be myself and express myself through the friends I made and the work I created as an art major in Arts High (I guess you can see that it was a big deal to me.)

At the time I was working at Planned Parenthood, a nonprofit organization that provides reproductive health services in the United States and internationally. The organization directly provides a variety of reproductive health services and sexual education, contributes to research on reproductive technology, and does advocacy work aimed at

protecting and expanding reproductive rights. I was working in the teen program funded by the organization. My boss, the director of the program, was named Maranda. She was a very intelligent, strong-minded, and compassionate woman. She wasn't about to let us make excuses or look for shortcuts (as I am sure many of us do or did in our teenage years from time to time)

One day, I came to work and everyone was talking about Parent and Teacher Night at our high school. Everyone was talking about how their parents would be meeting them at the school and about having them meet their teachers. I, on the other hand, just kept quiet and listened with excitement for them. Maranda asked me if I was also going and I told her that I was. then mentioned that I might not go because my parents aren't around. There was a bit of silence, but it didn't last long enough to make me feel uneasy.

Then she offered to go and play the role of my mother... None of my teachers had ever met my mother, so I was sure it would work.

Maranda asked me to stay after work so she could talk to me. When everyone left she asked if I really wanted to go and I gave her a nod with a yes. Then she offered to go and play the role of my mother. She said if that wasn't okay with me, she would accept my decision. But I really wanted her to attend with me, so I agreed. I made her promise not to tell anyone that she wasn't my mother. None of my teachers had ever met my mother, so I was sure it would work.

When we arrived to the school that night, everyone was in awe that my mother showed up. I remember my teacher saying, "This is your mother? She is beautiful." He began flirting with her, which made me laugh. Maranda would look at me and wink as she talked to my teachers and friends. She listened with such appreciation when she heard about the good things I did, and she would give me a real mother's frown when she heard of my playfulness and occasional lack of interest in certain classes.

I was full of excitement and appreciation for what she did. No one knew that Maranda wasn't my biological mother, but at that precise moment, she truly was my mother. We both walked out of the school with wide smiles. It was love in its purest form. As we stood outside the school, I watched her eyes tear up with gratitude and appreciation for the night. Friends and teachers walked out, saying, "See you on Monday, Rahfeal. Good night, Ms. Gordon."

After that, how could I not believe that people come into your life for a reason or season?

After that, how could I not believe that people come into your life for a reason or season? Maranda played a role in my life on that evening that hadn't been filled for almost four years. My mother didn't come to one parent-teacher night during my high school years, but that final year, she showed up.

The following weeks, Maranda asked me about my plans for after graduation and noticed that I was on the fence about college and where I was going to attend, ever since the negative statement by one of my counselors. So she put on her mother's hat and made me bring every college application I could get my hands on to work. Instead of coming to the teen sessions after school, she

directed me to an empty office and had me fill out those applications.

I applied to all the colleges and universities that sounded interesting and well known. I did not have good grades, but I did score well on the SAT. Every time I arrived home at my grandparents' house, we would eagerly waited to see which institution would be my destination. And then it came.

All the doubts that I wasn t going succeed were now irrelevant.

I was accepted to Montclair State University. I yelled and screamed, excited beyond reason. I showed my grandparents the letter, and they hugged me with equal joy. After everything I had experienced, I was going to college. All the doubts that I wasn't going succeed were now irrelevant. I was from the one of toughest parts of Newark, New Jersey, and I was about to be a college student.

The day after I found out, I went by the office where Maranda worked and shared with her the news. It was a blessed moment for me. I was going to college and one of my dear mothers was there to share in the moment with me.

TWO IN AND TWO OUT

As I entered college, I knew that I wanted to make an impact. I joined all the organizations I could, and I learned what was needed to make possible all the things I wanted. At the same time, I roughly adapted to college life because I didn't know about credit, financial aid, scheduling classes, and all the things that were expected from a freshman. I was accepted into college with the help of the EOF program, which I am so thankful and grateful to be one of their alumni. The Educational Opportunity Fund (EOF) provides financial assistance and support services (e.g. counseling, tutoring, and developmental course work) to students from educationally and economically disadvantaged backgrounds who attend institutions of higher education. The lessons the counselors taught me and the resources made available to me helped me realize the importance of an education.

I returned to Newark often because I still wanted to see old friends and family. My brothers were still in the hood, and despite my success, I refused to desert them. I remember being in my dorm when I received anonymous phone calls saying I should check on my brothers because they were causing mayhem in the hood. The phone calls caused me much stress, and I didn't know what to do.

I drove to Newark, and as soon as I arrived in the area, I came across an old childhood friend. I probably hadn't seen him in years, and I was surprised by his first words.

"Yo, your two brothers are off the hook. Those two dudes are wild boys. Someone is gonna have to calm them down."

My cousin was in the car and just looked at me when she heard his words. I knew she was wondering what he was referring to, but I didn't want to talk about it.

My cousin was in the car and just looked at me when she heard his words.

I took my cousin home, and I began searching for my brothers. I went to where they used to congregate and discovered that they were no longer on that side of the street. When I received updated directions, I immediately drove to the new location. As I approached the house they stayed in, I hopped out of the car and rang the doorbell. Alfonso answered the door, and he hugged me with his huge arms while Isaiah walked out nonchalantly. The three of us talked, and then I pulled Alfonso to the side.

I told him the situation and what I had heard, and he said he was loose (meaning not caring). But he told me not to worry because he would take care of Isaiah.

"You just do what you gotta do because you're in college. If you need us, you know how to find us."

I believed him. I knew that he would take care of Isaiah and keep him in his place because that's how it always was. Alfonso had Isaiah and I had Janvier. When I needed Janvier, he was there; when Alfonso needed Isaiah, he was there.

Our separate yet complete bond was known as two in, two out. Nobody could understand how the four of us could be so close but so distant in location. We all supported each other, but none of us was ready for the situation that was about to occur.

THE PROMISE

One day I decided to visit my uncle and hang out in the old neighborhood. I drove down the Garden State Parkway towards Irvington, New Jersey. When I arrived at my uncle's home, folks in the living room were planning a family reunion that was scheduled for July. I said hello to everyone, and I went to the kitchen for a drink. As I returned from the kitchen, my little brother Alfonso arrived through the front door. I was amazed at how big he had grown and how his dread locks were so long. We greeted each other as warmly as any brothers from the hood would do.

I decided to return to the kitchen to talk to Alfonso. He looked tired and stressed, and I could imagine what my 19 year old brother was experiencing in the hood. He told me that he stashed his clothes in the wall behind a 50 Cent poster and washed his clothes when our uncle wasn't home.

Alfonso then asked me to help him get an apartment, but I quickly declined because I knew it would be with drug money. I told him that he could stay with me, but he insisted that it was too far from where he needed to be. I

didn't want to become involved in the street life now, and I felt it would place me in a position where I didn't want or need to be.

Alfonso said he understood my decision and proceeded to walk out the door. I sat down and began eating some food, but it was tasteless. I started to feel as if I should be running out the door to talk to my brother. I knew he was returning to the corner where only two things happened, death and jail. I called him back down the street and expressed how I felt and how I needed him to change.

"You gonna have to be strong because you are going to be representing a lot of people who struggle."

"Hey big bro, if you make it on TV I will leave the street game. I will put everything down only if you call me and tell me you are on TV," Alfonso said.

I could tell he was serious by the tone in his voice.

"You are going to be big bro! But remember that these clowns are gonna hate. You gonna have to be strong because you are going to be representing a lot of people who struggle. They are going to be from the hood and from the top. We need a celebrity who represents the homeless and project babies like us," he continued.

He then said, "You told me to be the best man in whatever I do! And that is what I am going to do, be the best of the street game! Nobody really wants to help me, so I gotta do what I gotta do. They talk a good game, but they not real! You real big bro! You could have been a kingpin out here with all the people you know, but you chose to go to college and sell PARTY tickets rather than the color tops. And I respect you for that."

"Yo, big bro," he continued, "You are harder than most of these suckers out here. Those dudes you go to school with may never know our struggle, but they will soon from you. But keep that smile with a nation behind you as you tell our story! You gonna be big like Jay-Z and Puffy! I believe in you! I really believe in you!

I continued to listen intently.

"Big bro, I love you! And real talk, as you say, a man's words are weak if his actions are weak. If you make it on television, I will leave the street life alone and do whatever you say."

As my little brother walked up the street, I yelled, "Alfonso, don't go back there!"

"Fuck everybody else Rah! Just do you! But tell our story! If you don't tell our story, you will never be as big as you want to be! So just tell our story."

POWER OF FORGIVENESS

All of my college friends were getting ready to go to Miami for Memorial Day weekend. I wanted to go, but for some reason, I couldn't get myself together. I had never been to Miami while in college, and I made a promise to myself that this would be the year. I had my own apartment, a car, a full course load, and had the parties rocking for the college students. The spring semester was complete, and I was taking two summer courses while working as an intern with Enterprise Rental Car Service. I was doing well, yet I couldn't understand why I couldn't push myself to hang out with the college and local superstars.

My friends, including my roommate, left for Miami to enjoy the weekend festivities on Thursday and Friday while I stayed home. I made Ramen noodles and watched Law & Order the entire night. When I decided to go to bed, it was late. As I was getting ready for bed, I felt moody with many emotions, and my mind was in a state of dullness. However, I stilled managed to go to sleep quickly and gracefully.

Suddenly, it was very obvious why I did not go to Miami. I remember this day as if it were yesterday. At 4:23 a.m., I was awakened by a phone call from my cousin. I could hear the stiffness in his voice.

"He's dead Rah! They killed him Rah!"

My mind struggled to process the words.

"Calm down! Who's dead?" I asked.

> It has and will always be a moment that made me realize that life is full of surprises.

As he caught his breath, he replied, "They killed Alfonso."

My heart pounded and I began to cry as I never have cried before. I didn't sleep for days. I planned the funeral with my family. It has and will always be a moment that made me realize that life is full of surprises.

During my brother's funeral, I reflected on my brother's life and even made a statement that this could be the result when a child is not properly cared for. I also said that these situations can make you stronger or weaker. I chose to let it make me stronger.

As time passed, friends, acquaintances, police, and detectives called my family and me to see if we were okay. Additionally, I would stop by where my brother stayed from time to time. Alfonso had received love from many people, and to see that was very important to me.

Two months later, I received a call that the man that murdered my brother was apprehended and in custody. It made me feel good because we had so many people supporting the family to ensure justice was served.

At the same time, I started receiving letters as invitations to court hearings. I attended the listed dates to see justice for my brother's murder. Then I received a letter and a call about confronting the man who took my brother's life. I had so many things running through my head that I didn't know where to begin. I told the caller that I would want to meet him, and the court set a date.

As the date to meet my brother's murderer approached, some of my family discovered my intention to confront him. They advised me that I shouldn't go, but I felt it was necessary. At the time, I was working at the New Jersey Performing Arts Center in Newark. I didn't tell anyone at work what I was going to do on that day because I felt it was something that I had to do to move forward. I took my lunch break, and I headed to the court. When I arrived, I was escorted upstairs and met my grandmother who accompanied me for support. After my grandmother and I spoke for a while, the judge entered and the proceedings commenced.

The minutes seemed to go so quickly yet slowly as I waited for the moment to meet my brother s murderer.

The minutes seemed to go so quickly yet slowly as I waited for the moment to meet my brother's murderer. I had waited for this opportunity for the last two years. As the murderer entered the court room, he looked rough and rugged as though he hadn't slept since the day he was apprehended.

We soon discovered that the murderer was actually on trial for two murders. A family who sat in front of us was also victims of his sin; he had taken the life of their father, brother, son, and husband. Members of this family were the first to express their emotions to him.

Once they finished, I was told that it was my turn to confront my brother's murderer. As I approached the podium, I began to shake as many emotions stirred inside me. When I reached the front of the podium, the man was sitting down. I asked the judge to allow him to stand because I felt he shouldn't deserve to sit while I spoke to him. Once they allowed him to stand, I looked into his eyes and addressed him.

"You know, I have so much I want to say, but I don't think it will do any good. You took a life from this world. You took my brother's life who I loved with all my heart. I could curse you, but why? I just wanted to let you know that I forgive you for taking my brother's life. I truly, truly forgive you. As a godly man, I cannot hate you. I love you from the bottom of my heart. But best believe that you will have long days and longer nights. When you dream, remember my face and name. You have made me a stronger man, and because of your actions, I will become powerful. I pray that you find God while doing your bid and realize your sins. I thank you. I love you. And I forgive you."

I turned away and headed towards my grandmother. I kissed her on the forehead and told her that I was returning to work. As I walked back to work, I knew that my burden was lifted because I was moving as if I were gliding through the air with my wings widely spread.

I kissed her on the forehead and told her that I was returning to work.

WHAT YOU ARE SEEKING IS SEEKING YOU

After everything settled down after Alfonso's passing, I decided to leave school the following year. I was into my final year of college, but I was a complete mess. I was no longer interested in what was happening on campus, in my classrooms, with the social life, or with the events I was hosting throughout New Jersey.

Prior to leaving school, I wrote a one-page autobiography. Yes, I really wrote a one-page autobiography. So please hold your laughs—thanks! The document stated who I was, what I'd been through, and what I was willing to do to go to the top.

After I wrote the paper, I was able to have a friend edit it for me. I went to the computer lab on campus and printed about 100 copies. I put each one in a white envelope and sealed them tight. I didn't drive, so I took a bus down to the Newark Star-Ledger newspaper building. I stood in front of the building and passed out each envelope to anyone who walked into the building. I was determined to have

someone read or know my story. Security came outside and had me move away from the entrance, so I just walked to the side of the building and kept handing out those envelopes containing my one-page biography. I stood outside for hours until I had no more envelopes to hand out.

Nothing happened on that day. Not one person ran downstairs and said "your story is powerful." Not one person offered to drive me anywhere. Not one person offered to helped me pass out those envelopes outside in the cold. But that's how it is when you are trying to do the unthinkable, unimaginable, and extraordinary.

. . . I had no clue that what I was searching for was actually seeking me.

I remember calling one of my friends on the phone, upset. I'd had high hopes that someone would hear my cry or my call for help. I was seeking a way out of the pain, suffering, and looking for a way to heal the wounds that were invisible but deep. But even during my attempt to knock on the doors of the Star-Ledger, I had no clue that what I was searching for was actually seeking me.

As things were getting more hectic in my internal world, I had a feeling that something inside of me wanted to come out. I needed to get away to clear my mind, so I went to the home of one of my college friends. She always gave me a shoulder when I needed to talk. I explained to her all that was happening and she reconfirmed that things would get better. Just trust that God will provide was her message to me in so many ways.

As she went off to the kitchen to cook, I began watching MTV Jams with the volume muted. MTV Jams is a show that airs on the Music Television Video network that shows the most popular music videos in hip hop. I noticed that all they were showing was half-naked women, jewelry, cars, and as much violence that your brain can absorb through your eyes. I began yelling to my homegirl about what I was seeing on TV. I then asked myself, what if I could change the game in hip hop? What if, instead of being a rapper, I could be a motivational speaker in the hip hop world.

I then had the craziest idea: What if I could be a motivational speaker . . .

I then had the craziest idea:

What if I could be a motivational speaker who is as cool as Jay Z but as brilliant in business as a Bill Gates or Warren Buffett?

I said to my friend, "I want to inspire people to do big things and be great in life. Most of these dudes on television are actors; they don't know half this stuff. But what if I actually live a great life and I can actually teach and show people how to do it!?"

She thought it was a great idea and even said, "But you are already inspiring many people, Rah. You just don't see it all the time 'cause you are being you. I think that fits you perfectly. You should do it."

I pondered the idea as I went home, but I didn't feel it was the right time; I was still building up the courage to leave school.

When I finally made the decision, I attended my final class before actually leaving; it with my late mentor, Dr. Susan Weston. I adored her because she was always honest with me and gave it to me straight. As I was leaving her

class, she pulled me aside in the hallway and said, "I know you are going to pursue your personal goals and dreams and may just accomplish them all, but don't that get in the way of your education. You have to finish what you started. In this world, as a young African-American man, coming from what you've come from, you must finish. I'm a old Jewish woman telling you that you must finish your education, Rahfeal."

I truly adored Dr. Weston for pushing me to be more and do more. I told her I would definitely come back, but I had to pursue what my gut was telling me. Once I left, I had much more time on my hands. And that's when I started contemplating the idea of being a motivational speaker. The next and final chapter you are about to read will show you how the universe works and helps you find all that you seek.

THE GREAT ESCAPE

I went for every opportunity during my time away from school. I left not one stone unturned. I didn't want to live with regret about leaving school and not giving my all to my dreams and goals. I told a close friend that I could only rely on my faith and actions now. I didn't have the luxury of relying on my college degree, because I don't have one.

Things began to move along slowly, but nevertheless, progress was being made. I would network with everyone at every event I attended. I attended as many seminars, conferences, and workshops as I could with the free time I had. If I was going to nightclub events with friends, I would bring a book in my back pocket. You could catch me in VIP among people popping bottles, highlighting a sentence in the Think and Grow Rich book by Napoleon Hill. I was not playing any games. It was all or nothing

One day, I received a call from a friend who worked at BET, Eric Rhett. I always appreciated Eric for showing me love and support with the things I was creating on our campus at Montclair State University. He had called to

inform me that BET was having an audition for a show about college event planner/promoters. He thought it would be perfect for me. But the catch was, I had to submit my own audition tape via mail within the next two days. I didn't have a video camera and I didn't have anyone to film me. That didn't matter. I used every resource I could to get it done.

So this is how I did it . . .

- ✓ I was able to get a camcorder from a college friend.
- ✓ I set up in a conference room in downtown Newark that I paid for monthly through a virtual office service.
- ✓ I didn't have anyone to help film me, so I emptied the trash out of the conference room trash can, placed the can upside down, and put the camcorder on top.
- ✓ The TV producers called me to ask their interview questions and I was able to film myself while answering.

The next day, I sent the tapes out by next-day service and they had the tapes on the day of the deadline.

After a few weeks of waiting, I received a call telling me that I had been cast for the new television show. I was ecstatic. I celebrated with friends; things were on the way up for me. I was flown to Los Angeles to prepare for show. While in Los Angeles, I went to the L.A. Convention Center, where there was a business expo going on. It was there I met a young woman named Tove who worked for a magazine company called Black Enterprise. We exchanged contact information and stayed in touch during the period of my TV development.

But things never go quite as planned. When I returned home, I spent time with friends and family. I went to a park with a close friend to play basketball and ended up tearing my Achilles tendon. Because I wasn't able to walk, I couldn't continue on the TV show and I went into a deep depressive state.

Because I wasn t able to walk, I couldn t continue on the TV show and I went into a deep depressive state.

I lost the television show, dropped out of college, had no money from my event planning business, and I was back in the 'hood thinking there is no way out.

But God works in mysterious ways . . .

I still was in contact with Tove, who I'd met during my travels to Los Angeles for the TV show. She suggested that I pick back up the idea I'd had about becoming this new-generation speaker. She was starting a publishing company and thought it would be cool if I was her first client. So every day, I wrote a page for my book. It was a short book, but it was my short book. Once Tove read it, she said something was missing. She said I needed to tell my story. With her advice, I ended up writing two short pages and the introduction to the book.

I then decided to rent one of the theater rooms inside the New Jersey Performing Arts Theater (NJPAC). The reason why I chose NJPAC was because it was in my hometown. I was able to come up with the funding

with the support of my grandparents, friends, relatives, and churches I attended. The sold-out event was held on Thursday, September 21, 2007.

Tove wasn't able to publish and market my book the way that I wanted before my show at NJPAC. But what she did for me in spite of the failed project was an extraordinary blessing. She helped me establish and invest in creating my own publishing company (RahGor Publishing & Co.) with book distribution serving more than 39,000 retailers, libraries, schools, internet commerce companies, and other channel partners.

In the midst of all this, I was able to connect with a editor from the Star-Ledger who, two years prior, had written a story on Alfonso and his brothers. The journalist passed me along to another writer named Carrie, who interviewed me multiple times at a cafe in downtown Newark (I had handwritten my first book at that same cafe). Once she finished, the only thing left was receiving a call about when the article would come out.

I had handwritten my first book at that same Cafe.

My event was in September 2007, the interviews were conducted in October and November of 2007, the publishing company was finalized in December 2007, and on February 3, 2008 . . . I was on the front page of the Newark Star-Ledger newspaper.

And that's when I knew . . . .

My Location Was Not My Destination.

MY LOCATION IS NOT MY DESTINATION

There are many things that I could say to you as the reader who is trying to understand my story. You may have questions in your mind about certain parts of my life about what you may have read or heard. But my story is nothing more than an example that no matter who you are or where you come from, you can make it. I have so many stories that I omitted, but maybe it's because the ones that I felt moved me to a new level had to be documented. You may or may not have been to my seminar, but one thing I want you to remember is that we stand alone most of the time when we begin to move towards our purpose in life. Not many people will agree with you, but you must constantly believe in yourself. You must push, walk, crawl, run, drive, fly, and climb to your spot in life. I now understand what it truly means to have grace and favor. I was able to understand through my personal struggles I endured. So always be yourself and know that there is

no one like you. Your path is YOUR PATH. Walk that path however you see fit. If I never met you, just know that I truly love you. You can make it because through it all, I have and will continue to do so.

THE STRATEGIES FOR SOLUTIONS

The following are 23 strategies to help you find solutions if you are experiencing similar issues to what I went through in my life. As I share these strategies with you, please know that you MUST have unbreakable faith. You also must have an EXTREMELY diligent work ethic in order for these strategies to work for you. Let no one tell you that you can't get out of your situation (especially if he or she is in the same negative environment with you).

You were born to be great in your path. You were created to live, love, and laugh. Don't get me wrong; we all face storms in our lives, but there are rainbows afterwards. The individuals who see the rainbows are the ones who danced in the rain when others cried in the puddles.

STRATEGY

Find mentors who are successful in your career area or the career area in which you desire to enter. Ask to spend fifteen minutes with them or have lunch with them once a month. When you have confirmed a mentor or mentors, ask questions and listen to their advice. These are the people who want to see you succeed and help remove you from your struggles.

STRATEGY 2

Keep a journal to write or type your emotions. Writing is therapy that soothes the pain in your soul. When no one wants to hear you, vent on that paper or keyboard. Don't bottle up your feelings because it will hold you back. Think of a journal as a Band-Aid for a cut; it helps the healing.

STRATEGY 3

Read books that have information to help you create the lifestyle you want (or remove you from a negative environment). These books are in categories that are titled "Self-Help." There are many books on numerous topics, but you should center on the books that build character, motivation, and focus on subjects that cater to what/who you want to become. If you want to be a doctor, read books from the medical field, but you should also read books that focus on personal development as well.

STRATEGY

Find something for which you would die. This may seem like an extreme statement, but think about a person (could be you) who lives in an extremely negative environment where people are dying every day around them because of the evils of the street. You have to double your positive energy just to get through each day of living in that toxic situation. The goal is to have a POWERFUL "WHY". Why do you want to leave this toxic environment? Are the reasons so that you can live past 25, to start a family, and not have to worry about losing one of them before 18?

STRATEGY

When your window of success is open, you must work harder, faster, and stronger because that window will not remain open forever. It will open and close at various times.

STRATEGY 6

Become aware of what keeps you from taking the right steps and being resourceful. Then you must stop it.

STRATEGY

There are many opportunities that will come your way, but you must understand that every opportunity isn't for you. When you have a clear focus on your mission, select the opportunities that will be beneficial to help accomplish it.

STRATEGY

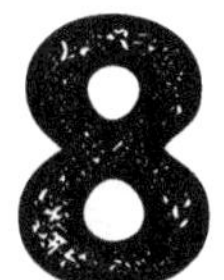

Make quantum leaps in your life. To do this, you will have to visualize yourself as already being successful. In other words, pretend you have already achieved your goal. You need to become that person on the inside, and then you will attract success into your life. The reason why visualization works is that the unconscious mind cannot tell the difference between what is real and what is imagined. So if you imagine something, your mind makes it real and brings it to reality.

STRATEGY

Spend at least ten minutes in front of the mirror every morning describing who you are for the day. Examples: I am amazing; I am a great business person; I am an honor roll student; I am going to be a college student; I am the best father/mother for my children.

STRATEGY 10

Take trips to the areas where you want to live. If you remain in an environment that you don't enjoy for a long time, you can be in a depressed state of mind. It is best to visit environments that make you happy, relieves stress, or where you can imagine living.

STRATEGY

Slowly remove fear, anger, shame, and guilt because they are forms of toxic emotions that cloud your ability to perceive the truth. This hurts relationships because when you have these emotions, a person you may need in your life will not be open with you.

STRATEGY 12

Intensify what you can do and find individuals who can intensify what you can't.

STRATEGY

13

Plan an exit strategy. Research and plan before you make major moves. If you take the time to do both of these things, you will get out of anything and won't have to worry about going back.

STRATEGY

Don't tell everyone your plans because you may have many crabs around you, and they will want to keep you down with them. Just work hard and smart! Don't worry about what others are doing. You have to get out of where you are.

STRATEGY 15

Find programs that can help you get the things you don't have. These programs can focus on getting a college degree, high school diploma, a trip out of the country, insight on how to start a business, or how to be the best at a particular activity. No matter what the focus may be, make sure you find as many programs and resources as possible.

STRATEGY 16

If your inner circle is not challenging, you will have to change the people inside. You MUST stay among those who will challenge you and inspire you to live better.

STRATEGY

Act as if you are already where you want to be. The mind will attract all the things to you that you think you are. Always remember you are what you think. Don't think negatively because the mind will connect you to all negativity and keep you in a negative environment.

STRATEGY 18

Challenge and make goals for yourself. It is very important that you set goals that excite you but at the same time make you work hard to build what you never had.

STRATEGY

Create a vision board. Take a poster board and paste pictures and words that define your future and who you plan to be. Keep this in a place that you will see it every single day. Use magazines and old books to cut out these pictures. This vision board is to help you see the future!

STRATEGY 20

Think about the worst that could happen before you make a decision. You may have already started making changes in your life, so you have multiple opportunities coming your way. Remember that every opportunity that comes your way isn't always good for you. Think things through and then make a decision. If you have to make an emotional decision, us your gut as it will never steer you wrong.

STRATEGY 21

Read daily positive affirmations and articles that are inspirational. These readings will help trigger innovative ideas to make your life more positive.

STRATEGY

22

Ask for help when needed. Do not have too much pride to ask for help when struggling. You will get to the promise land, but you can't get there all by yourself. You need assistance and guidance. Those willing to help you get there are the ones you should treasure like gold.

STRATEGY 23

When things get really dark and it seems that there will be no light, say, "My location is not my destination." Repeat it over and over again until you are balanced and have a grip on yourself. It is a MUST to give yourself self-motivation because there will be times in your life when no one will be around. It will only be you and the thoughts in your head. However, you will get through because you are special, and you already know this. Embrace the struggle, and it will take you to personal freedom.

RAHGOR
DAILY AFFIRMATIONS

Directions: Say one affirmation twice each day. Once in the morning and once before you go to bed. You MUST say these affirmations to yourself in the mirror with confidence. After each one, say, "I can and I will." This will help you get in a positive state of mind to make daily personal changes. Be good. Live prosperous.

DAY

Today, I embrace change in my life.

As I continue to grow and blossom in the field of life, I will be the reflection of beauty. Today, I spread the purest love I hold within. Today, I move mountains, split seas, and align the stars within my universe to receive all that I envision.

DAY

Today will be AMAZING. I will command the attention of every eye in the room because of the godly spirit that is within me. I will smile more today than I did yesterday. I will say thank you more because today I receive more. Today my lifestyle has more value and my life has more meaning!

DAY

Today, I attract WEALTH and PROSPERITY. I am money magnetic, and all forms of prosperity look for me. Today, I CLAIM valuable gifts, job bonuses, checks in the mail, increases in savings accounts, and amazing increased percentages on the stocks in which I have invested. I SPEAK PROSPERITY over my life today, and all those who are attached to me will prosper. Today, I become increasingly rich in financial numbers and wealthy in financial intelligence.

DAY

There is no one I would rather be than I! I claim greatness and all the deepest forms of love to be within my life. Today, the world will show me love, and I will show it back double time. I am more than average today. I am the complete form of amazement and beauty.

DAY

Today, I am completely FREE and the creator of my destiny. For the next 10 years, I will defy the laws of gravity and not give into the "chicken mentality" of the world. Today, I am an EAGLE that knows it was created to fly high! Today, I see my omens and thank the heavens for what they have and will be sending me!

DAY

Today, I walk my dreams down the aisle to marry them. I am changing their last names from (say your first name) dreams to (say your first name) goals. Today, I plan to accomplish and enjoy them with the little time I have on this earth. Today, I marry my visions, my passions, my desires, and my true happiness.

DAY

Today, I CLAIM THE EXTRAORDINARY! I claim that new car! I claim that new home! I claim having the children I always wanted! I claim that wife/husband! I claim joy, happiness, peace, positive energy, and love! I claim that college degree! I claim that job position! I claim a better life than the one I have now! I claim what will make me happy because I was not born to struggle nor be unhappy in this AMAZING LIFE! Today, I claim and change for the better.

DAY

Today, I plant the seeds of forever. I will leave my mark on the hearts of family, friends, and strangers. Today, I will show the next generation how to survive when they become the old generation. I will enjoy this moment so that when it becomes the past, I can enjoy it as a memory in the future. Today, I will be what I will be remembered for when I am no longer here.

DAY

On this day, life has given me diamonds and pearls to share with all those who are around me. I feel so blessed to be given complete access to the treasures of the world. Today, I walk with intense faith as I move forward into the unknown hours of today. I may not know what the total day will bring, but I do know that I bring gifts of love, peace, joy, style, and enthusiasm. Today, I am wealthy in mind, body, and soul!

DAY 10

Today, I am stepping out on my faith. I cannot be scared if I am excited for what I am pursuing. I am on this earth for a certain mission and one purpose. Today, I move closer to my purpose by completing my missions. I am far from where I came, and that means I can DO THIS! Today is here, and today I have NO FEAR!

DAY

11

Today, I smile because I lost count of all the many blessings I have received in my life. Even though I am flawed, I have so many people who accept me for who I am. Today, I celebrate with smiles and positive gestures. Today, I give kisses, handshakes, hugs, eye winks, and text messages that end with a smiley face. Today, I am just thankful for my life.

DAY 12

Today, I love myself just the way I am. I know that there are BILLIONS of people in the world, but there is no one like me. Today, I laugh more, smile more, hug more, kiss more, and dance more. I will make this day feel like the LOVE I want to experience every day. I am who I am, and those who accept me for who I am will know who I am.

DAY

13

Today, I will focus on being a better person than I was yesterday. I forgive those who left me, hurt me, lied to me, and neglected me. I am MORE than what others believe I am. Today, I will capture the love that is created in moments. I will smile at happiness and hug joyful situations. I, (say name), am grateful for all I have experienced, and I am looking forward to being a great experience to someone else.

DAY

Yesterday is where I will leave all my troubles. In yesterday, I prayed for a day of change, and that day is TODAY. I claim that my storm is over! Today, I turn my wrongs into rights. I leave behind unhealthy relationships, harmful eating habits, imperfections, negativity, darkness, and immaturity in the days of YESTERDAY. I embrace love, positivism, God, balance, light, new relationships, and the smiles of my guardian angels.

DAY 15

Today, I have ENORMOUS faith! I am moving the TALLEST mountain and moon walking across the WIDEST ocean in my life. Today, I am equipped with the tools to FIX the problems and build the foundations needed in my life. Today, I SPEAK into the world the things I want to see and who I want to be.

DAY

16

Today, I know better so I will do better! What I believe will be conceived and received. Today, I think twice but will speak once. My seeds of yesterday are sprouting today! So I will continue to water it with pure love, powerful thoughts, positive words, and positive energy!

DAY

17

Today, I receive all within the all.

I will send out positive compliments to all those I know because a compliment is another glue that holds relationships together. Today, I intensify my love and passion towards life. This day has arrived, and TODAY, I will do nothing but be thankful to be ALIVE!

DAY

I am just the most amazing and unique person on the planet. I control my emotions and thoughts today. I am climbing mountains and breaking down walls in my life with ease. Today is my life without any boundaries!

DAY

19

Today, my dreams flirt with my reality. I will allow myself to enjoy the true intimacy of life. Today is sexy because I am sexy. I will be more tempting to those who lay eyes on me because my spirit is attractive. Today, I walk on water as I allow my life to put on a fashion show for all those who meet me today.

DAY 20

Today will be simply beautiful. My positive thoughts and blessings will flow like the Nile River into my garden of life. I will glow brighter so that my kids, friends, and family members will always have a light to see. Today, I will be all I can be within all that I see and surround me. Today is simply beautiful because I am.

DAY 21

Today, God dwells within me as me.

I will allow my light to shine from the highest mountain upon the cities (people). Today, I am radiant and simply powerful. Today, I leave alone the scabs of the past so that my healing process can completely pass.

DAY

22

Today has nothing to do with what has already happened. Today is the exact seed I need so that I can grow tomorrow. I will be open for financial gain and wisdom today. I will be who I want to be today so that I will not have regret tomorrow. Today, I claim great health, wealth, and prosperity in my life!

DAY 23

Today, I am just amazed at how fine, beautiful, handsome, sexy, and radiant I am! Today, I will think BIG and smile BIG. Today, I will walk like a king/queen because my life was crowned with GREATNESS. I will get rid of those who are toxic and think like peasants. I cannot waste my time that is just as valuable as rubies and gold! Today, my life is BLAZING and AMAZING!

DAY 24

Today, I claim QUANTUM LEAPS in my life. I move forward with a peace of mind. I will receive so many blessings today that my mouth will hurt from saying THANK YOU. I will be the light for the children who are in darkness, and I will be the smile that my family and friends need today. I am sexy, I am wonderful, and I am God's beautiful masterpiece!

DAY 25

Today, I embrace change in my life.

As I continue to grow and blossom in the field of life, I will be the reflection of beauty. Today, I preserve my sexiness while spreading the purest love I hold within. Today, I move mountains, split seas, and align the stars within my universe to receive all that I envision!

DAY 26

Today will be AMAZING. I will command the attention of every eye in the room because of the godly spirit that is within me. I will smile more today than I did yesterday. I will say thank you more because today I receive more. Today, my lifestyle has more value, and my life has more meaning!

DAY

27

Today was created with doors to wealth and opportunities. Today, I will walk into any room and illuminate it with my spirit. I am more handsome, sexy, brilliant, amazing, and determined than I was yesterday. Today, I will let nothing hold me back because I am great, and great people only move forward!

DAY

28

Today, I claim QUANTUM LEAPS in my life. Today will be better than it was yesterday. I will allow wealth, love, healthy relationships, blessings, and happiness to enter my life today. Today, I turn impossible into I'M POSSIBLE!

DAY 29

Today, I will be able to unlock the doors to my new life. I have packed up all my old issues and shipped them to God's hands. Today, I will be shopping for new things to make my house (life) as comfortable as it can be. Today, I am excited for the new memories I will be creating within my life. I am excited for all those who will enter my life to enjoy the house warming. Today, I close and become the owner of the house I always wanted.

DAY

30

Today, the secrets of life will be revealed to me. I am becoming wealthier in mind, body, and soul. Today, the secrets to success will be told to me. The more I seek for success, the more it will show itself to me. Today, my life is the complete example of Laws of Attraction.

DAY 31

The words I speak today will become my reality. The words I speak today will manifest right in front of my eyes. Today, I will speak things into existence with my gift of words. I speak prosperity today! I speak great health today! I speak achievement today! I speak a career promotion today! I speak life into the world of those who lost their souls! I speak happiness within my family today! I speak longevity and legacy over my life today! Today, I speak blessings into the world!

www.ingramcontent.com/pod-product-compliance
Lightning Source LLC
Chambersburg PA
CBHW072012040426
42447CB00009B/1597